# 79.4 WAYS TO CELEBRATE YOUR OLD AGE

Wit and Wisdom for the Savvy Senior

# 79.4 WAYS TO CELEBRATE YOUR OLD AGE

Wit and Wisdom for the Savvy Senior

# JANET LAIRD
"Queen of the Dingbats"

Omaha, NE

© 2014 Janet Laird. All rights reserved. No part of this book may be used or reproduced by any means, graphic, electronic or mechanical, including photocopying, recording, taping or by any information storage retrieval system without the written permission of the publisher except in the case of brief quotations embodied in critical articles and reviews.

Pick A Daisy Press books may be ordered from your favorite bookseller.

Pick A Daisy Press
c/o CMI
13518 L. Street
Omaha, NE 68137


ISBN: 978-0-9849305-3-1 (paperback)
ISBN: 978-0-9849305-4-8 (Kindle)
ISBN: 978-0-9849305-5-5 (EPUB)

Library of Congress Control Number: 2013923558


Designed and produced by Concierge Marketing Publishing Services.
Printed in the USA


10 9 8 7 6 5 4 3 2 1

With family at one end, friends at the other and God in the center, life is an amazing road trip.
>	— Janet Laird

# DEDICATION

This book is dedicated to my grandchildren: Matthew, Adrian, Rachel, David, Randy, Michelle, Todd, and Cora. I pray that you will enjoy the present and have no fear of the future.

The quotes from "Mama Said …" are from the book by my favorite aunt, Lois G. Harvey. She was gracious enough to give me permission to use her work.

# INTRODUCTION

The ideas in this little book have been popping in and out of my brain for quite some time. I finally decided to write them down after observing a group of seniors crowded together in one room eating potluck and getting reacquainted after many years of separation. As I searched the room for familiar faces, I noticed the difference in expressions from one countenance to another. Some appeared happy while others had that "I wish I were far away" look. As the afternoon wore on and I visited with those long-lost friends, I began to realize that the happy faces were not only happy at the moment but the souls behind them seemed happy with their everyday lives. The people who wished to be elsewhere appeared to be looking for some unknown place so they could finally find contentment. They probably won't live long enough to find that elusive spot because nirvana is a state of mind, not an actual location.

The real joy in life comes from those everyday little happenings that we tend to take for granted or overlook completely. If we don't relish these little pieces of our existence as they come along, we often feel bored and fail to appreciate most of our life experiences. When my children said they were bored, I told them, "Only boring people are ever bored." This applies to adults as well.

That said, here is my list of *79.4 Ways to Celebrate Your "Old" Age*. The fact that you are lucky enough to be able to read and comprehend this book gives you a distinct advantage over many seniors. If you are able to express your thoughts—good or bad—after reading these ideas, you are even farther ahead of many of your peers. The fact that you even *want* to find more ways to celebrate is a testimony to your mental acuity. Say a prayer of thankfulness and enjoy the book. These ideas are not meant as medical advice, but as advice from a voice of experience. Use what fits into your life and schedule, and dismiss all the rest. The exact number of suggested ways was determined by adding the 2010 U.S. life expectancy from the Centers for Disease Control and Prevention of both men and women who had lived to at least age 65 and then dividing by two.

These *79.4 Ways to Celebrate Your "Old" Age* are not in any particular order because as I age I find myself thinking random thoughts. My daughter asked me if I was losing my ability to multitask, and I had to admit that at this point, I am lucky to task at all. So, here they are just as they came to me. Enjoy!

## # 01

# "OLD" AGE

**"OLD" AGE** is at least two years older than you are right now. Don't "think" yourself old before your time. We all know people who seem to have been born old and some who will be forever young. You can make a conscious decision about the category in which you will live. One friend told me that you are not old as long as you know someone who is older than you. She is 92 and knows someone who is 103, so of course she does not consider herself old yet. If you are under 70, you are a pediatric geriatric. At 70 you become a geriatric. At 80 you are on your way to "old" age. Only you can decide when you have finally reached that destination.

# # 02

# AGE IS A STATE OF MIND

**AGE IS A STATE OF MIND.** Young at heart doesn't mean wild and reckless. It is the ability to enjoy the moment. Once we forget how to laugh at life and ourselves, we are old. Have a hearty laugh every morning because laughing is good for both your mental health and your lungs. Can there be a better way to start the day? I have a funny little stuffed "thing" sitting on my desk that says "Press me" where the heart should be. When I press it, it laughs hysterically in a child's voice. The day I don't laugh with it is the day they should take me away.

# # 03

# GET A NEW HIP

**GET A NEW HIP**, or knee, or whatever procedure you need. Take care of your health. Don't let fear keep you in pain. If your doctor says it's "time," then be brave. Bite the bullet and do it.

## # 04

# REMEMBER TO TAKE YOUR MEDICINE

**REMEMBER TO TAKE YOUR MEDICINE.** Put it in a weekly planner, and keep it where you eat your meals. Forgetting meds is one of the biggest problems we seniors have. They cost too much to forget, and the consequences can be dire.

# # 05

# TAKE YOUR VITAMINS

**TAKE YOUR VITAMINS.** If you have trouble swallowing those big pills, you can purchase chewable or gummy vitamins now. Not only do we need the multivitamin, but some extra C and D are also helpful. Ask your doctor about taking an 81 mg. ("baby") aspirin every night to help avoid that dreaded stroke or heart attack. I remember when most doctors told us that if we ate right we didn't need vitamins. That way of thinking seems to have changed, especially with geriatric doctors. As we age, we often find it difficult to digest some necessary vegetables; and even when we do eat the right foods, our bodies do not always use and process them correctly.

# 06

## SAY "NO" WHEN YOU NEED TO

**SAY "NO" WHEN YOU NEED TO.** We can find ourselves doing things that we know we don't have the energy or strength or mental ability to do just because we were asked and didn't know how to say "No." We forget that younger people often don't realize our limitations and expect us to continue doing what we did 10 years ago. There is nothing wrong and everything right about saying, "I wish I could help, but I just can't do that. Maybe I can help in a different way."

# 07

# WRITE A BOOK

**WRITE A BOOK.** What are your credentials? Are you qualified? Think of it this way: You have lived, loved, worked, and known good health and ill health. You have earned money, spent money, and been both wise and stupid. You have been happy and sad, succeeded and failed. You have been kind and you have been mean. You have been generous and stingy. You have been jealous and also forgiving. *This is the human condition.* What part of your humanity can you share that might make life easier or encourage someone else? Will knowing about your career help someone who is struggling for success? Will sharing an experience give someone a laugh? Will understanding your faith help someone who is searching for grace? Will my sharing *79.4 Ways to Celebrate Your "Old" Age* bring a smile or an idea to someone I don't even know?

# # 08

# WHEN WOMEN TRAVEL

**WHEN WOMEN TRAVEL**, wear a beautiful red hat, a purple scarf with a sparkly brooch, and your best smile. You will attract positive attention and be offered assistance with any needs you may encounter. It pays to dress up when you travel. So many people look like they just finished pulling weeds in the garden or running in the park with the dog. Whatever your age and wherever you are, being well-groomed and neatly dressed is always a plus. Leave those expensive pieces of jewelry at home. Hide them or leave them with a friend or family member, and only take items that you would not miss if they were lost or stolen. After all, whom are you trying to impress?

# # 09

# WHEN MEN TRAVEL

**WHEN MEN TRAVEL,** they get good results in a loud Hawaiian shirt and a jaunty hat. Don't forget that winning smile. Many a travel experience has turned into a disaster because of pickpockets. Find out how to protect yourself and take precautions. A money belt is an excellent idea, and remember to keep your wallet in your front pants pocket. Carry your camera in a case around your neck and put some extra money in one of the pockets in the camera case or wear a passport case under your shirt. While you are sightseeing during the day, leave valuables in the safe in your hotel room. Take along only the amount of money you want to spend that day so if it is lost or stolen you won't be broke. Also, it's a good idea for each person traveling to have a separate credit card in their own name. Never put money or your passport in your luggage or carry-on.

# # 10

# DECORATE YOUR WALKER

**DECORATE YOUR WALKER.** Everyone I know absolutely hates his or her walker. But if you have to have one, at least make it cute. Entwine a fake rose vine up and down one leg or put pompoms on the outside of your basket. Add a bicycle horn to alert folks when you are trying to get through a tight spot. Appreciate what that walker does for you. You have mobility and a convenient place to sit when necessary. Instead of hating it, enjoy the freedom it gives you. Others are not as conscious of it as you are. In fact, if you stop complaining, they will forget all about it.

# # 11

# NAME YOUR CANE

**NAME YOUR CANE.** If you are female, give it a male name. I saw a woman in an airport searching around her seat. I was close enough to hear her say, "Thomas, where are you? You're never here when I need you." A short time later, she found and grabbed "Thomas" and they marched off. I don't know if Thomas was the name of her deceased husband or an old boyfriend, but just from that one sentence I knew she was an interesting lady. I wished we'd had time to visit. Can you imagine a man with a cane named Marilyn? You know he would be a fun guy!

# # 12

# WHAT IS THE NAME

**WHAT IS THE NAME** of your car? Mine is Gertie, and I find that she gets better gas mileage if I talk nicely to her. We have named our cars since my childhood, so I forget that not everyone has a personal relationship with his or her vehicle. It seems that cars with names are kept cleaner and have more regular maintenance than ordinary vehicles. Anything that costs that much money deserves a name, even if it is the name of the banker who gave you the loan. Our culture names everything because we have such a variety of similar items. When someone says, "Oh, you smell so good," you don't say, "It's my perfume." You say, "It's 'My Sin'" or "It's 'Polo.'" Certain backless high-heeled shoes are known as "Hello, Sailor" shoes. Names are an inexpensive way to spice up your life. Use your imagination and your personality will shine through everything you do. And, don't forget to buckle up in your car!

# # 13

## HAVE A BIG "SURPRISE" BIRTHDAY PARTY FOR YOURSELF

**HAVE A BIG "SURPRISE" BIRTHDAY PARTY FOR YOURSELF.** The surprise part comes when you give your kids the bill. Many times, kids wait until we are too old to really enjoy a party. So, do it yourself while you still have lots of friends on this side of the grass, and you can all enjoy a good time. I was just kidding about the bill. Have as much of a party for yourself, your friends, and family as you can afford. As my mother always said, "Don't save it all for the nursing home."

# # 14

# GO ON A CRUISE

**GO ON A CRUISE.** Once on the ship, you don't have to get off until you are back at your home port. Seeing new places is fun, but just being on the ship is vacation enough for many of us. Don't feel like you have to "do everything" to have a great time. You'll get your money's worth from the food alone. If walking is no problem for you, then get out and see the world. But don't stay home and moan because walking is a problem. There is nothing like an early morning sunrise over the ocean. Even if it's close to home, everyone should see a sunrise at least once a year. So the next time you wake up early and can't get back to sleep, go out in your back yard and watch as the day begins. At least look out the window!

# # 15

# PUT A LITTLE ROMANCE IN YOUR LIFE

**PUT A LITTLE ROMANCE IN YOUR LIFE.** Send someone flowers. Sign the card, "Your Secret Admirer." No one is ever too old for a secret admirer. Hey ladies, it isn't just men who can send flowers. Wouldn't your spouse enjoy a "secret admirer"? You wouldn't have to tell for a few days or maybe never. *"If a man wonders if he is in love, he probably is. If a woman wonders if she is in love, she probably isn't."* (From "Mama Said …" by Lois G. Harvey)

# # 16

## TAKE A GRANDCHILD TO THE CONCERT OF HIS/HER CHOICE

**TAKE A GRANDCHILD TO THE CONCERT OF HIS/HER CHOICE.** You will be grateful for your hearing loss. It may cost you big bucks, but your grandchild will always remember that experience with you. Keep a smile on your face at all times, and say how much you enjoyed going! When they are middle-aged, they will realize what a gift it was!

# # 17

# GET INTO THE MODERN AGE

**GET INTO THE MODERN AGE.** Get a computer or iPad. Take classes and learn how to use the device. Get a cell phone and text your grandchildren. They will be so proud of you! You *can* learn new things. Even if you do remember the days before television, it doesn't mean that you are stupid. You may not be able to do it as well as an 8-year-old, but you *can* do it! My theory has always been that kids are so good at technology because they just push buttons to see what will happen. We, on the other hand, worry about breaking the darn thing. We know how much we paid for it, and we don't want to mess it up. Kids have no concept of cost and just want to see what it will do. We need to be a little more like them in that way and just "Go for it."

# # 18

# HAVE A PASSION

**HAVE A PASSION**. Become an expert on something or someone. Did you always want to know more about the Civil War? Have you always wondered about Queen Victoria? With computers, all this knowledge is at your fingertips and it is easy and fun to do research. Also, with a Kindle you don't even have to worry about where to store the books.

# # 19

# FIND A *NEW* HOBBY

**FIND A *NEW* HOBBY**, something different than your past hobbies. Keep the old, but add something new. You will be amazed at what you can do if you just try. Many seniors have discovered an unrealized talent for painting. Get some paint and take a class. The first time you walk into a classroom after so many years really is a scary moment. But once you are settled in and begin to meet the other students, it becomes fun. Each time, it becomes easier and more rewarding. Maybe you won't be another Grant Wood, but if you think about it, one Grant Wood was enough. You just might want to have the fun of holding a brush, mixing colors, and making something uniquely yours. Don't let fear keep you from experiences that can add so much to your life.

## # 20

## TAKE CLASSES IN SOMETHING THAT INTERESTS YOU

**TAKE CLASSES IN SOMETHING THAT INTERESTS YOU.** Community colleges have "Continuing Education" classes in almost everything. They are so reasonably priced that they are almost giveaways to seniors. How about calligraphy, or dog obedience classes for your critter, or a photography class? If you can't find anything that interests you, then maybe you need an attitude check. Don't become the biggest bore in your family. Leave some interesting memories for your children and grandchildren.

# # 21

# BAKE COOKIES

**BAKE COOKIES.** This is especially good for men. Cookie mix is available in a box and frosting is available in a can. Add eggs, oil, and water. It not only makes the house smell good, but it improves the attitude of anyone in the vicinity—spouse included. If you take a dozen cookies to your next oil change, you can be sure they will remember you when you call for your next appointment. It's a good way to guarantee top-notch service. Get in the habit of taking a dozen cookies when you go visiting or to the doctor or dentist. Apartment dwellers know they get prompt service if the maintenance workers know they will be rewarded with a dozen cookies.

# # 22

## IF YOU ARE LUCKY ENOUGH TO HAVE A SPOUSE

**IF YOU ARE LUCKY ENOUGH TO HAVE A SPOUSE**, give him/her a "Good morning" and a "Good night" kiss every day. When you live alone, it is almost impossible to get that human touch connection, and it is sorely missed. So, if you have a spouse or partner, don't waste that opportunity because you truly are one of the lucky ones. Sometimes it is necessary to forgive past indiscretions before you are able to be comfortable with intimacy. Be the big person and forgive. You will receive more than you give. *"You should be at least as polite to your family as you are to your friends."* (From "Mama Said …" by Lois G. Harvey)

# # 23

# **PLANT SOMETHING**

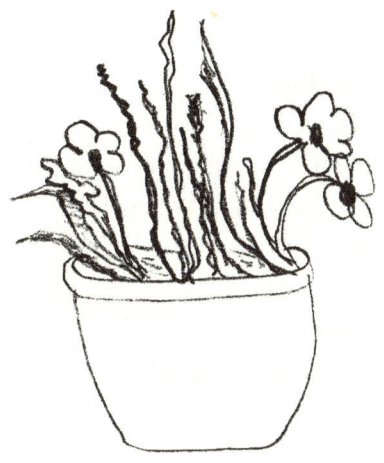

**PLANT SOMETHING**, even if it is just in a flowerpot. Take care of it and watch it grow. Be sure to talk to it daily because experts say it is important and does make an actual difference in the plant growth. So if you live alone you can talk out loud all day long and, if you are overheard, you can always say you were just talking to your plant.

# # 24

# MAKE YOUR PEACE

**MAKE YOUR PEACE.** Define your belief system. Write it down. If you have questions, which many of us do, talk with a spiritual leader. Read the Bible. *"There are only five prayers worth saying: We praise thee, Lord. Thank you, Lord. Forgive me, Lord. Help me, Lord. Into Thy hands. And if you can say the last one sincerely, the others are not necessary."* (From "Mama Said …" by Lois G. Harvey)

# # 25

# MAKE YOUR ARRANGEMENTS

**MAKE YOUR ARRANGEMENTS.** Write your own obituary because if you leave it to others, they won't get it right. Put in only what you want known. Tell your children that you wrote it, and give them and the funeral home a copy. Make your own funeral arrangements and pay for them. This will ensure you will get what you want and will assure your family of this without burdening them with decisions at an emotional time. Pay for your casket, otherwise your family may pay more for it than you paid for your first house! If you want to be cremated, now is the time to make sure it happens.

I know a man who planned his funeral right down to the food served afterward. He planned a morning service so that instead of just finger foods, his family and friends had a full noon meal of turkey, dressing, and all the trimmings catered in from a local restaurant. He said he was so thankful for the life he had been given that he wanted to serve a Thanksgiving Dinner, but he didn't want the women of the church to have to cook. They did serve it, and he left the church a generous gratuity for their work. So, even though it was March, his family and friends celebrated his life with Thanksgiving.

# # 26

# THINK BACK TO YOUR CHILDHOOD

**THINK BACK TO YOUR CHILDHOOD.** Write a story titled, "My Favorite Aunt" (or Uncle). Tell everything you know about him or her and why that person was your favorite. Leave this with your important papers so that your children will find it. It is a piece of family history that will get passed on. If you feel really ambitious, write a family history of all the old family stories that you were told. I qualified mine with this statement: "I don't know if these stories are true, but this is what I was told, so enjoy them and pass them on."

# # 27

# WRITE EACH OF YOUR CHILDREN AND YOUR SPOUSE A LETTER

**WRITE EACH OF YOUR CHILDREN AND YOUR SPOUSE A LETTER.** Do it now while you are feeling well. Tell them the fun things you remember about living with them. Be sure to mention how proud you are to be their parent. When you finish, you will be on a roll and can even write to each of your grandchildren. Just think how much you would enjoy a special letter written just to you from your spouse, your parents, and grandparents. Seal each of them and give them to the funeral home to pass out after your funeral. If you were remiss as a parent or a spouse and for whatever reason it is impossible for you to atone for your shortcomings while you are alive, now is the time to write an apology. You will never know if you were forgiven, and maybe that is best.

# # 28

## CHECK OUT THE MEMORIAL CARDS USED BY YOUR FUNERAL HOME

**CHECK OUT THE MEMORIAL CARDS USED BY YOUR FUNERAL HOME.** I know a woman who had her picture and a quote on the front of hers. The picture was so lifelike because she was smiling her biggest smile. The quote said, "I just want everyone to know that I had such a good time." Just from that information, don't you wish you had known her? What do you want yours to say? Do you want someone else to decide?

# # 29

# GET ENOUGH EXERCISE

**GET ENOUGH EXERCISE.** Doctors encourage us to walk. Well, that can be dangerous both from a balance point of view and from a criminal point of view. So, many seniors join walking clubs and walk in groups at the mall. Some get their exercise working in the yard or garden. Apartment dwellers often walk the halls. You will improve your health if you can find some way to walk 30 or more minutes a day. Remember, it doesn't have to be all at one time.

# # 30

# MIRROR MESSAGES

**MIRROR MESSAGES** help start your day in an upbeat fashion. I have two messages on mine: *"Good morning, God"* and *"Smile." "Good morning, God"* starts my daily prayer while I brush my teeth and get myself ready for the day. I don't say "Amen" until I am in bed and ready for sleep. That way, I stay in prayer and can continue any time during the day. My most common daily prayer is, "Lord, help me keep my mouth shut." Starting the day with a big *smile* helps me remember that everyone is always better looking with a smile. *"Just before you go to sleep each night, think about what the best thing was that happened to you all day."* (From "Mama Said …" by Lois G. Harvey)

# # 31

# HOW ABOUT TAI CHI?

**HOW ABOUT TAI CHI?** These classes are excellent for both men and women because we all need help with balance. It is a slow exercise with deep breathing and excellent for seniors with COPD. If no classes are offered in your area, they can be purchased on a DVD and done in the comfort of your own home. Not only will your body benefit from the exercise, but your mental attitude will improve because of increased oxygen to your brain.

# # 32

# VOLUNTEER

**VOLUNTEER.** Schools always need people to listen to children read. The boys especially like to have a man be their reading "buddy." Elementary schools still are pretty much a "woman's world," so having a man interacting with the children is a real treat. Many boys need a Grandpa figure, and you just might make a difference in a life that no one else could make. *Where* isn't as important as the *doing*. Just be sure that you enjoy it. If not, find another place. If you have the right "fit," you will get much more than you give.

# # 33

# GIVE A PROGRAM

**GIVE A PROGRAM** at a Scout meeting, in a classroom, or at a Sunday school. What can you teach the boys and girls of today? Were you in the Navy? Show them how to tie knots. Do you love to fish? Teach them how to make a lure, and tell them your most exciting fishing experience. Can you bake a pie quick as a cat can wink its eye? Everyone has something to teach young people if they will just take the time to do it. Imagine how much our youth would learn if every adult they knew taught them something useful or wise. They would not only learn, they would feel cared for. Isn't that the way it is supposed to be? If the old don't teach the young, who will?

# # 34

# CLEAN OUT A DRAWER A DAY

**CLEAN OUT A DRAWER A DAY.** Throw away everything that is out of date. Nothing is more confusing to your children than finding papers, bank books, and insurance policies that are not valid. They have to spend time and sometimes money to see if they are relevant.

## # 35

# YOU ARE OLD ENOUGH TO BELIEVE IN DEATH

**YOU ARE OLD ENOUGH TO BELIEVE IN DEATH.** Teenagers don't think they will ever die, but you, on the other hand, should have realized your mortality by now. Act like it. Clean house. Put all important papers in a fireproof box and label it as "Important Papers." Don't be like the television commercial where the husband says, "*If* something happens to me ..." Duh, of course something will happen to him. Why don't younger people realize that we have faced the fact that we will die, and it's not all that earth shattering? Talk to your children about your demise. You have so many choices to make. Make ones that will help your descendants deal with your death and remember you for your wisdom.

# # 36

# TALK TO YOUR HEIRS ABOUT YOUR WISHES

**TALK TO YOUR HEIRS ABOUT YOUR WISHES.** Make a will. Many families have been divided by dumb things. One family even split over the division of Grandma's handkerchiefs. You will feel so good when you have everything in order, and your children will be forever grateful.

# # 37

## LAUGH EVERYDAY

**LAUGH EVERYDAY.** Get some DVDs of Red Skelton, Carol Burnett, Bob Hope, Johnny Carson, the Three Stooges, or whoever you remember that made you laugh. A good laugh is not only good for your mood, but good for your lungs. Laugh often, breathe well! The really talented comedians don't need the "F" word.

# # 38

# GET IN THE HABIT OF MAKING LISTS

**GET IN THE HABIT OF MAKING LISTS.** There's nothing wrong with giving our memories a boost. It's better to have a few notes than to forget important appointments. Sticky notes are great because you can leave yourself a message on your mirror or on the inside of the door so you will see it as you are leaving the house. Have a dish where you *always* put your keys, and then when you want to take books back to the library, return an item to the store, or mail letters you just put them on top of your keys and you won't forget them.

# # 39

# KEEP A LARGE CALENDAR

**KEEP A LARGE CALENDAR** and write on it every night before going to bed. Where did you go? Who called? Who did you see? Any unusual aches or pains? What do you have going for tomorrow? Any doctor appointments? Bills due? Speaking of bills, why not have the bank pay them automatically? A couple of the advantages include that they are never late, and you can be on vacation and not have to worry about paying them from a distance. Calls to make? Set yearly goals and put them on the last page of the calendar. Refer to them on the first day of every month and check them off as you reach them. How about that ten pounds? Gone by July? Good for you. How about the family reunion? Still working on that one. Christmas shopping done? Funeral arrangements made?

# # 40

# WHAT SONG DO YOU LOVE

**WHAT SONG DO YOU LOVE** to hear because it makes you happy? Learn the words and make that your morning song. It doesn't matter if you sing well, you just need to sing! I know a man who has sung a morning song since he was a teenager. The song changes as he ages, but he can still remember and sing each one. Singing is not only good for the soul, but also the lungs.

*The bear went over the mountain* 🎵

# # 41

## MANY OF US FIND THAT AS WE AGE WE HAVE THE PATIENCE OF A GNAT

**MANY OF US FIND THAT AS WE AGE WE HAVE THE PATIENCE OF A GNAT.** Maybe it is because we have a limited time left on this earth, and we don't want to spend most of it waiting in line. We all know someone who has always been late for everything. We have put up with it for years. It is OK to remind them that our patience is limited (with a smile, of course). As for waiting in line, force yourself to think happy thoughts and do not complain to those around you. It makes me wonder why stores think we want to shop at their establishment and then wait to give them our money. I try to go to stores that don't play music and that do hire enough employees to service their clients. Some restaurants make me grumpy because they are so noisy. They aren't designed for conversation to begin with (high ceilings and bare floors), and then they play music. Who goes to a restaurant to listen to loud music and yell at friends?

# # 42

# LEARN TO PLAY A FEW CARD GAMES

**LEARN TO PLAY A FEW CARD GAMES** and get together with friends. One man said, "Cards are something to hold in my hands while I visit with my friends." Most games can be learned in an afternoon, and it is well worth the effort. Time spent with friends keeps us young. The older we get, the more interaction we need. Depression is a serious illness among seniors, and spending too much time alone is one of the main factors that lead to depression.

# # 43

# PLAN ONE MENU

**PLAN ONE MENU** that you can feed family and friends. You can make it yourself or order in. Freezers are especially wonderful for entertaining. First you microwave to thaw, and then you microwave to cook. Invite people to lunch or dinner at least once a month. It is definitely worth the effort and gets easier every time you do it. Don't think the house has to be spotless before you invite guests. Do you check out the houses when you are invited to dinner? If so, you are not being a friend. There is nothing as much fun as a man who loves to cook. I remember when a brother-in-law was making chili and added a candy cane right off the Christmas tree. Great chili! We will remember it, and him, with a smile until the day we die.

# 44

# MAKE A SPECIAL EFFORT

**MAKE A SPECIAL EFFORT** to find an old friend or two. Maybe there is someone from grade school that you remember fondly. With the Internet, you can find almost anyone. Ask a grandchild to help you. When you locate them, give them a phone call or write a letter, and let them know what you remember that makes them special to you. You never know how you might brighten someone's life.

# # 45

# IF YOU WERE LUCKY

**IF YOU WERE LUCKY**, you had a mother or grandmother who insisted there was a place for everything and that everything be in its place. Now is a good time to practice that old rule. Tripping over something and taking a fall is a very real danger. Falling can ruin the rest of your life. This is not the time to live in a cluttered house.

# # 46

# PETS CAN BE WONDERFUL COMPANIONS

**PETS CAN BE WONDERFUL COMPANIONS**, but they can also be a tripping hazard. Love them, but be careful. If they become a burden, find them a good home. Many people are looking for older dogs in order to avoid the puppy stage. The same applies to cats.

# # 47

## IF YOU CAN AFFORD IT

**IF YOU CAN AFFORD IT,** join a gym and hire a "personal trainer." Be the healthiest that you can possibly be. Have your doctor's consent, and make sure your trainer is aware of your limitations. This will not only make you stronger, it will force you to get up and out at least three mornings a week.

# # 48

# FIND A SENIOR CENTER

**FIND A SENIOR CENTER** that you enjoy, and go once a week or more for the activities and lunch. If you have a spouse, be that cute couple that is always ready for fun. If you are single, you can still be cute and fun!

# # 49

# TRUST YOUR INSTINCTS

**TRUST YOUR INSTINCTS.** If you are seeing a doctor or other professional and feel uncomfortable, trust yourself. Find another. Ask for a second opinion. One privilege of age is that we have experience on our side. Don't allow yourself to be bullied by professionals who are supposed to be caring for you. Sometimes, they don't.

# # 50

# TAKE A TAXI

**TAKE A TAXI** to an evening event if there is something you really want to attend, but you don't drive at night. Don't miss that speaker or band from your past just because you can't drive downtown. Have the cab drop you off right at the door. Then use that new cell phone to call when you are ready to be picked up. Spend some of your hard-earned money on yourself. You will enjoy it more than it will be appreciated by whoever gets it.

# 51

# GET YOUR HAIR DONE

**GET YOUR HAIR DONE.** Humans feel better when they know their hair is styled. Try a different look and color. Color is for anyone who wants it, both men and women. It's only hair. If you don't like the color or style, it will grow out and you can change it again. I know a man who visited his mother in the nursing home and left thinking that it was probably the last time he would see her alive. He went to visit friends and lamented her sad state. He hardly slept that night waiting for the nursing home to call and tell him that she had passed. No call. In the morning he went to see her. Her bed was empty. He found her in the beauty shop getting the perm she had previously scheduled. She was bright-eyed, happy, and very much alive.

# # 52

## BE VERY CAREFUL

**BE VERY CAREFUL** if you get a manicure or pedicure. Pay close attention to their sterilization process. If in doubt, don't. A nail fungus or infection can be almost impossible to cure. A diabetic should never get a pedicure. Soak your feet at home and have your podiatrist clip your toenails. If a technician ever nips you and draws blood, bring it to his or her attention and don't go back to that person. One of the safest places for both is a cosmetology school that is teaching both the techniques and sanitation processes.

# # 53

# TAKE SWIMMING LESSONS

**TAKE SWIMMING LESSONS.** If that sounds like too much, you can at least do water aerobics. It is fun and good for you. Both men and women gain strength and balance and enjoy the classes.

# # 54

# SEE A DERMATOLOGIST

**SEE A DERMATOLOGIST** for a skin cancer checkup. If you live alone, you have no idea what is behind you! This is equally important for both men and women. You need a professional opinion for those strange skin spots that we all get as our skin goes through its many stages from baby to adult and beyond. The "beyond" part gets especially interesting. Don't waste your time worrying; instead, get it checked.

# # 55

# FACE THE HARD FACT

**FACE THE HARD FACT** that there is little you can do to change the world or the people you love. You can vote. You can encourage people. You can give to the needy. That's about it. Pray for them and stop worrying. Your time is too limited to waste it lamenting over circumstances out of your control. I'm grateful that I'm on my way out instead of the way in. Everyone thinks his or her generation was the best, and that is as it should be.

# # 56

# WHAT ABOUT MONEY?

**WHAT ABOUT MONEY?** Will you run out? At $7,000 a month for a nursing home, most of us will run out if we live there very long. And who wants to do that? Yet don't deny yourself every pleasure because you are saving it for the nursing home. I don't advocate being careless with your funds, but you do deserve to be warm in winter and cool in summer. Some seniors try to save money by skimping on heat and air conditioning. You are not wise if you endanger your health. If money is a concern, please don't be embarrassed to ask for assistance. You paid taxes for years. If you need a little back now, so be it. You deserve it.

# # 57

# HOLIDAYS

**HOLIDAYS.** Remember how much fun Christmas was? Your children were young and believed in Santa Claus. Remember the Sunday school program where they were dressed as angels and wise men? Then they grew up and Christmas became a gimme-gimme free-for-all. Now you have children and grandchildren with way too much "stuff." Try a different approach this Christmas. Ask everyone to get together and take food to your local food pantry, or ask each family to purchase gifts for a family that is truly struggling to provide for the basic needs of their children. Those who still believe in Santa Claus should still get gifts,

but everyone else can spread cheer to others who are in need. Ministers will be eager to help you find families and many churches and schools have "giving trees" with hand-written needs hanging from them on slips of paper.

# # 58

# MY FATHER

**MY FATHER** reminded me that the difference between being considered eccentric versus crazy is the amount of money one has. It was his way of telling me that I didn't have enough money to wear fuzzy rabbit ears at Easter while visiting him in the hospital. He didn't understand what a great relief it was to finally get to the point in your life when you no longer care what people think, and you can just be who you truly are.

# # 59

## DON'T GOSSIP

**DON'T GOSSIP.** Remember what your mother said: "If you can't say something nice, don't say anything at all." It's bad enough to be a gossip, but to be an "old" gossip is really over the top. By the time we are seniors, we should know better. Men are definitely not exempt from this. *Never forget to be truthful and kind. Hold these virtues tightly. Write them deep within your heart.* (Proverbs 3:3)

# 60

## BE CREATIVE

**BE CREATIVE.** It is human nature to be creative. We all have that gene because of the necessity to improvise our way through life. If we don't have what we want or need, we make something else work for us. Bake and decorate something. Let your imagination flow. You are unique, so bake, paint, or build something that is uniquely yours.

## # 61

# WHAT ABOUT ALL THOSE OLD PHOTOS

**WHAT ABOUT ALL THOSE OLD PHOTOS** from your parents and grandparents? If you don't know who they are, throw them away. You can be certain that your children and grandchildren won't be interested in looking at pictures of people no one knows. Pick out the best pictures of your relatives, and label them for your heirs. Throw the rest away.

# # 62

# HAVE A MORNING COCKTAIL

**HAVE A MORNING COCKTAIL** of two tablespoons apple cider vinegar in a big glass of water. Vinegar can be used as a cleaning agent, so in your mouth and throat, it helps kill bad bacteria. During cold and flu season, another dose at night is also helpful. Another plus is that you are getting two of the eight glasses of that water we often forget to drink. Enjoying this cocktail is an acquired taste.

# # 63

# NEED SOMETHING EASY TO TAKE TO POTLUCKS?

**ESPECIALLY FOR MEN: NEED SOMETHING EASY TO TAKE TO POTLUCKS?** Here is a recipe you can make and have in the refrigerator for weeks:

**BETTY'S PICKLES**

Purchase 1 quart of dill or any pickle. Drain, rinse, cut into bite-size pieces, and put back in the jar with ½ teaspoon pimento. Bring the following to a boil: 1 cup sugar, ½ cup white vinegar, ½ cup water, 1 teaspoon celery seed, and a couple garlic cloves. Put the jar in the sink. Put a butter knife in the jar with the pickles, and pour the boiling mixture on the knife. This will keep the hot liquid from breaking the jar. Carefully remove the knife after all the liquid is in the jar. Let cool. When cool, put the lid on and refrigerate for at least four days before eating. When it is time for the potluck, put the pickles in a nice old-fashioned pickle dish that you bought for $1.98 at a thrift store. Wrap with aluminum foil and you are ready to go. You can honestly say that you made the pickles yourself.

# # 64

# HAVE A GIFT DRAWER

**HAVE A GIFT DRAWER.** This is especially good for men who don't enjoy shopping. Ask your granddaughter to go with you the first time. Get a supply of gift cards and bags. Purchase nice bath soaps, a beautiful brooch on sale, or a pretty candy dish. Put these in your gift drawer where you already have the cards and gift bags. Once you get an eye for specialty items, you can be ready for any occasion. This is an easy way to be a very thoughtful, special man. A man once told me that he had never bought a gift for anyone. His wife always took care of everything. If she wanted a Christmas present, she had to buy it for herself while shopping for the children. There was a hint of pride in his voice. Poor man never knew what he had missed. *"We make a living by what we get. We make a life by what we give."* (Winston Churchill)

# # 65

# CHECK OUT PAWN SHOPS

**CHECK OUT PAWN SHOPS.** If the price is right and you like it, does it matter where it came from? This applies to jewelry, musical instruments, and more. Often pawn shops aren't in the best part of town, so you may want to go with a friend. My son took me the first time, and I now go with lady friends as it is in a safe part of town and two nice women work there. I have purchased two of my favorite rings at this shop. I paid $15 for one, and it appraised at $300. Love a bargain!

# # 66

# VISIT THRIFT AND ANTIQUE SHOPS

**VISIT THRIFT AND ANTIQUE SHOPS.** Like pawn shops, they are an interesting way to spend an afternoon, and you may just find something that you will enjoy for years. Even when you don't make a purchase, the experience of seeing items from your past that you had forgotten about brings back a flood of memories. When I saw an old dipper, I remembered the pail of water in the kitchen. We all used the same dipper. I was just a kid so I don't know if we had more colds back then because of it, but I do know that we didn't go to the doctor unless we needed stitches or had broken a bone.

# # 67

# RIDE A MERRY-GO-ROUND

**RIDE A MERRY-GO-ROUND.** Take a child if you aren't brave enough to go alone. You don't have to ride an animal because there are benches for us older folks. Go around and around and enjoy the music while remembering experiences from your youth at fairs and carnivals.

# # 68

# MARK BIRTHDAYS

**MARK BIRTHDAYS** on a large calendar, and get a supply of cards at the dollar store. Write something on the card that could only come from you. No one could write on a birthday card better than my dad. He always let me know that he was proud of my efforts. Your children never tire of hearing how much they are loved and how they make you proud.

# # 69

# MEET YOUR NEIGHBORS

**MEET YOUR NEIGHBORS.** Do more than just wave. Take over some cookies. Turn your light on for trick-or-treaters. Invite your neighbors to join you on the porch swing. Sponsor a neighborhood potluck supper. There was a time when all the neighbors knew each other. The women had morning coffees, and the whole block got together for cookouts. When the women of the house started working outside of the house, it became too much trouble to be neighborly. What a shame. Do your part to keep the neighborhood acquainted.

# # 70

# GROW SOME HAIR ON YOUR FACE (FOR MEN ONLY)

**GROW SOME HAIR ON YOUR FACE (FOR MEN ONLY).** Not a full beard, but some. Gray hair on a man's face is especially attractive on some men. You won't know until you try it. By now you have learned that if it doesn't look good you can just laugh at yourself and shave it off. If it looks good, you have a new look. Comments from friends and family will let you know if it is a flattering style. At least you'll know, and wisdom is our goal. Check out the popular styles in men's magazines. You are never too old to have that "devil-may-care" look. Of course, women should have their facial hair waxed or a laser treatment done.

# #71

# TAKE A NAP

**TAKE A NAP.** Some people enjoy a 20-minute "power" nap in their recliner. Others need a couch, pillow, and blanket for at least an hour. Whatever your choice, do rest during the afternoon. If you are worried that you will sleep too long and have trouble sleeping at night, set a kitchen timer for 20 minutes, and see how that works for you. A nap early in the afternoon is better than falling asleep while trying to watch evening television and definitely ruining your night's sleep.

# #72

## WRITE SOMEONE AN ACTUAL LETTER AND MAIL IT

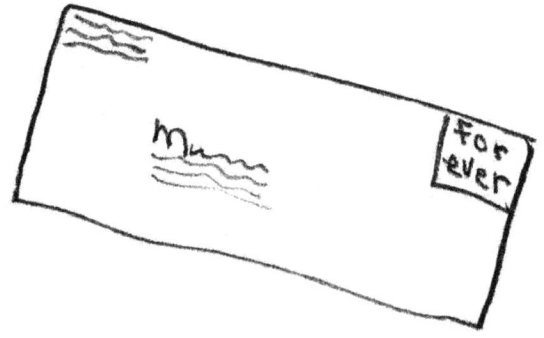

**WRITE SOMEONE AN ACTUAL LETTER AND MAIL IT.** The easiest way is to send a birthday card with a handwritten letter inside. Use a piece of stationery, not the inside of the card. Make it a real, old-fashioned letter. You will make someone feel extra special.

# # 73

# ASPIRE TO BE WISE

**ASPIRE TO BE WISE.** One way is to read the Book of Proverbs in the Bible. When you have finished, *"Read the whole Book of Luke in the Bible and you will know just about the whole story."* (From "Mama Said ..." by Lois G. Harvey)

# 74

# GET YOUR TEETH WHITENED

**GET YOUR TEETH WHITENED.** Your dentist can do it, or you can do it at home. It is a good idea to check with your dentist first because he or she may be able to sell you a stronger strength than you can buy at the drugstore.

# # 75

# PAPER OR PLASTIC?

**PAPER OR PLASTIC?** Always choose plastic because cockroaches love brown paper bags and can move into your home before you know it. What to do with the plastic bags? If you are of a creative bent, check out the Internet (especially www.pinterest.com) because it is full of craft ideas. If not, you can recycle them at a grocery store or give them to your local thrift store.

## # 76

## KEEP SCISSORS HANDY WHEN YOU READ YOUR NEWSPAPER

**KEEP SCISSORS HANDY WHEN YOU READ YOUR NEWSPAPER.** Newspaper, coffee, and scissors—the perfect morning combination. After you cut out items of interest, drop them in a manila envelope and once a month sort through them. I have a special file where I put the obituaries of people I know, a special recipe box for recipes to try from the paper, and another file for comic strips and news stories that I want to keep. When I am ready to send a birthday or get-well card, I go through my stash and see if it contains anything that person would enjoy. Some comics and articles just seem to remind me of certain people, and when they receive one, they know I was really thinking about them.

# # 77

# VISIT YOUR FAVORITE COUSIN

**VISIT YOUR FAVORITE COUSIN.** With so many couples having only one child, that leaves many without cousins. I can't imagine that because I have 32 first cousins. Even with that many, I have one favorite. We are the closest in age and share growing-up memories. I love to visit Diane in California and enjoy her visits back to the Midwest. E-mail has been such a blessing for us.

# # 78

## CALL YOUR MOTHER

**CALL YOUR MOTHER.** I was lucky enough to have my mother for almost 69 years. Everyone should be so lucky. If you can't call Mom, call everyone else you love just to tell them so. Whether or not they love you back is beside the point. Being able to love without needing confirmation is your reward.

# # 79

# SAY A DAILY PRAYER

**SAY A DAILY PRAYER** of Thanksgiving. Twice a day is even better. Counting your blessings keeps your life in perspective.

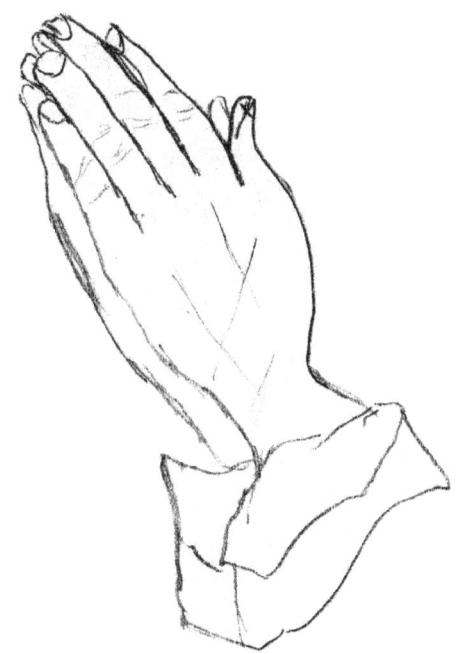

# .4

# **KEEP SEX ALIVE**

Whether actual or in memory, sex is better now because...

# ABOUT THE AUTHOR

This is Janet Laird's second book on enjoying the life you have been given. Her first book, *"Surviving Widowhood with Maggie Montclair and Friends,"* was written especially for widows but also was read by widowers who later wrote the author to ask her to write a book directed toward them. They said they were just as lost as widows. As every woman knows, it is often difficult to see situations from a man's point of view, thus *79.4 Ways to Celebrate Your Old Age* became a reality. These suggestions are for all smart and savvy seniors, male or female, from age 55 years and beyond.

Janet was born and raised in Oelwein, Iowa, and is a graduate of Upper Iowa University. She currently lives in Omaha, Nebraska, and still travels as much as possible with her family and her Red Hat

Society chapter, "The Dingbats in Red Hats." Janet is working on a children's book and also collaborating with several authors and illustrators on a special edition storybook for families.

As we age, and we all do, it is time to take stock and prepare for the inevitable. That doesn't mean we can't go out with flair. Determine what you want your legacy to be, and make it happen! Live while you still can!

*It is true — there really is life after the death of a spouse.*

Surviving widowhood is no easy task, but with practical Maggie and feisty Gertie along for the ride, it suddenly doesn't seem as daunting anymore!

AskMaggieMontclair.com

www.ingramcontent.com/pod-product-compliance
Lightning Source LLC
Chambersburg PA
CBHW022122040426
42450CB00006B/798